The Twelfth Chester Book of Motets

Christmas & Advent Motets for 5 voices

Edited by Anthony G. Petti

LIST OF MOTETS

CHESTER MUSIC
(A division of Music Sales Limited)
14/15 Berners Street, London W1T 3LJ, UK.

ORIETUR STELLA

A star shall rise from Jacob, and a man shall spring up out of Israel. He shall destroy the leaders of alien peoples, and the whole earth shall be his possession. All the kings of the world shall adore, every nation shall serve him.
(Based on *Numbers, 24 , xvii*)

Jacob Handl (1550-91)

4

* alto and tenor interchanged from 33, iii–36, i.

ALMA REDEMPTORIS

Kind mother of the Redeemer, the open gateway to heaven and star of the sea, help your fallen people who strive to rise again; we pray you, who bore your holy Son by a miracle of nature, a virgin first and last, who received God's greeting from the mouth of Gabriel, have mercy on sinners. (Attrib. Hermann Contractus)

Orlandus Lassus (1532-94)

CANITE TUBA

Sound the trumpet in Sion, for the day of the Lord is near. See, He is coming to save us. Winding paths will be made straight and rough places smooth. Come, O Lord, and do not delay. Alleluia (*Joel,* 2 , i; *Isaiah,* 40 , iv).

Giovanni Pierluigi da Palestrina (1525-94)

*There are various possible solutions to the problems of *musica ficta* in bars 17-19. The most cautious is simply to sharpen the tenor F, bar 18.

*The syllables-'nas:' and 've-' are set below the succeeding F and D respectively in the original.

*This syllable is set below the succeeding B♭ in the original.

O SAPIENTIA

O wisdom which comes from the mouth of the Most High, extending strongly from pole to pole, which orders all things fittingly: come and teach us the way to be prudent.

Robert Ramsey (c. 1590-c. 1644)

fór - ti - ter, suá - vi - ter - que dis-pó - nens ó - mni-a, suá - vi - ter - que dis-

fór - ti - ter, suá - vi - ter - que dis-pó - nens ó-mni-a, súa - vi - ter - que dis-

fór - ti - ter suá - vi - ter - que dis-pó - nens, suá - vi - ter - que dis-pó -

fór - ti - ter, suá - vi - ter - que dis-pó - nens ó - mni-a, súa - vi -

fór - ti - ter, suá - vi - ter - que dis-pó - nens, suá - vi -

-pó - nens ó - mni - a: ve - ni ad do-cén-dum nos vi - am pru-dén - ti-

-pó - nens ó - mni - a: ve - ni ad do-cén - dum nos vi - am pru-dén - ti-

-nens ó - mni - a: ve - ni, ve-ni ad do-cén-dum nos vi - am pru-dén - ti-

- ter - que dis-pó - nens ó - mni - a: ve - ni ad do-cén-dum nos,

- ter-que dis-pó - nens ó - mni - a: ve - ni ad do-cén-dum nos,

BEATA VISCERA

Blessed is the womb of the Virgin Mary, which bore the Son of the eternal Father. Alleluia.

William Byrd (1543–1623)

SURGE ILLUMINARE JERUSALEM

Arise, shine, Jerusalem, for your light has come, and the glory of the Lord has risen upon you (*Isaiah, 40, i*).

Francesco Corteccia (1504-1571)

24

TRIA SUNT MUNERA

There are three precious gifts which the Magi brought the Lord.

Juan Esquivel (late 16th-early 17th cent.)

O BEATUM ET SACROSANCTUM DIEM

O blessed and most holy day on which Our Lord deigned to be born of the Virgin Mary for our sake. Let the whole world therefore rejoice, and let us sing to him to the sound of the trumpet, strings, the harp and the organ. Let us rejoice with the numerous hosts of angels ceaselessly singing his praise. Noel, alleluia.

Peter Philips (c.1561–1628)

cí - - tha - ra, psal-té - ri - o et ór - ga-no, psal-té - ri - o et ór - ga-no.

cí - - tha - ra, psal-té - ri - o, et ór - ga-no, psal-té - ri - o et ór - ga - no.

psal-té - ri - o et ór - ga-no, psal-té - ri - o et ór - ga-no.

cí - - tha - ra, psal-té - ri - o et ór - ga-no, psal-té - ri - o et ór - ga-no.

psal-té - ri - o et ór - ga-no, psal-té - ri - o, et ór - ga-no.

con - gra-tu - lé - mur e - xér - ci - tus, e - xér-ci -

con - gra-tu - lé - mur cum mul-ti-tú - di - ne an - ge - ló - rum e-xér-ci-tus, e - xér - ci -

con - gra - tu-lé - mur cum mul-ti-tú - di - ne an - ge - ló - rum e-xér-ci - tus, e - xér-ci - tus

con - gra - tu - lé - mur cum mul-ti-tú - di - ne an - ge - ló - rum e-xér-ci - tus, e - xér-ci - tus

con - gra-tu - lé - mur cum mul-ti-tú - di - ne an - ge - ló - rum e-xér-ci-tus, e - xér-ci -

HODIE CHRISTUS NATUS EST

Today Christ is born, alleluia. Today the Saviour has appeared, alleluia. Today on earth the angels sing and the archangels rejoice, noel. Today the just exult, saying: glory to God in the highest, alleluia, noel.

Jan Pieterszoon Sweelinck (1562-1621)

* It is suggested that $\downarrow$ in $\frac{6}{4}$ and $\frac{3}{4}$ = $\downarrow$ in ¢ and $\frac{2}{4}$ throughout.

* alto and tenor lines interchanged from 21, i, to 24, penultimate note.

Printed by Caligraving Limited Thetford Norfolk England

The aim of this present series is to make more readily available a comprehensive body of Latin motets from the Renaissance and Early Baroque periods, combining the inclusion of old favourites with the provision of lesser known or hitherto unpublished works. Generally speaking, all the pieces are within the scope of the reasonably able choir. They also encompass a fair selection from the liturgical year as a guide for use both in church and in the concert hall when performing choirs wish to present their programme according to theme or a particular season.

The editor has endeavoured to preserve a balance between a critical and performing edition. The motets are, where necessary, transposed into the most practical performing keys, are barred, fully underlayed, and provided with breathing marks. They also have a reduction either as a rehearsal aid or as a form of accompaniment, since at least some of the works of the later period were clearly intended to be reinforced by a continuo. Editorial tempi and dynamics are supplied only in the reduction, leaving choirmasters free to supply their own in the light of their interpretation of a given piece, vocal resources and the acoustics. The vocal range is given at the beginning of each motet. Also provided is a translation of every text and a table of use.

As an aid to musicologists, the motets are transcribed, wherever possible, from the most authoritative sources, and the original clefs, signatures and note values are given at the beginning and wherever they change during the course of a piece. Ligatures are indicated by slurs, editorial accidentals are placed above the stave, and the underlay is shown in italics when it expands a ditto sign, or in square brackets if editorial. Where the original contains a *basso continuo*, it is included as the bass line of the reduction. Figurings are not included, however, because they are usually extremely sparse, and do not normally indicate any more than the harmony already provided by the vocal parts. Finally, each volume includes a brief introduction concerning the scope of the edition, with notes on the composers, the motets, and the sources, together with a list of editorial emendations and alterations, if any.

This volume contains nine motets from the sixteenth and seventeenth centuries, four of them for Advent, and five for Christmas, and is intended as a companion to volume 6. Some attempt has been made to provide not only a variety of text but also a fair sampling of different styles and a reasonable degree of national representation. Thus the selection comprises two English composers (one a Catholic exile on the continent), one either English or Scottish (Robert Ramsey), two Italian, one Dutch, one Flemish, one Slovene, and one Spanish. There is also the usual attempt to balance the familiar and the unfamiliar in this selection.

The seasons of Advent and Christmas are well served by Renaissance composers, both in quantity and quality of settings. Though Advent cannot rival Lent and Holy Week in profusion of texts and music, its liturgy encompasses a wide range of moods, combining penitence, wistfulness, expectation and excitement, all of which seem especially appealing to Renaissance composers. As for Christmas, it continued with the dominant popularity to which the Christmas carols and villanescos had already testified. By comparison, the feasts of Easter, the Ascension and Pentecost do not seem to offer the same personal appeal, for all their doctrinal importance and liturgical prominence. Certainly, when one tries to recall the best known masterpieces of Renaissance polyphony, the Christmas motets strongly figure amongst those which most quickly come to mind: Byrd's *O magnum mysterium* (volume 6) and *Ave verum* — at least associated with Christmas (volume 2); Handl's *Resonet in laudibus* (volume 6); the two eight-part motets of Palestrina, *Hodie Christus natus est* and *Surge illuminare* (the latter published individually by Chester); Sweelinck's *Hodie Christus natus est* (the present volume); and, perhaps most famous of all, Victoria's *O magnum mysterium* (volume 6).

The first composer in this collection, Jacob Handl (1550-91), sometimes known by the Latin form of his name, Jacobus Gallus, was born at Reifnitz, Carniola, but spent most of his life in Bohemia. He was a member of the court chapel for a time, then chapelmaster to the Bishop of Olomouc, but from about 1568 spent the rest of his life in Prague. Handl's style varies considerably. He wrote large-scale works using double choirs in the Venetian manner, and intricate, harmonically sophisticated motets with abundant chromaticism; but he could also write entirely chordally in a simple and highly economical vein. *Orietur stella*, like all the other Handl motets in these volumes, is mainly within this last category, and is similarly both easy and rewarding to sing. It was published as no. 13 of *Tomus primus musici operis harmoniarum*, Prague, 1586 (copy in the British Library). A motet of great sonority and rhythmic vitality, it skilfully alternates the chordal (as in the opening) with the mixed or free style (as at "et exsurget homo" and "possessio eius"). The homophonic is most forcefully used in the triple section depicting the crushing of alien leaders. There are other touches of word-painting, as with the ascending phrase for the rising star (bars 1-3) and the large leaps on "exsurget" (bars 10 and 11). The motet also has modal and tonal interest, rarely staying within its ostensibly Dorian mode.

Orlandus Lassus (1532-94) is known by various forms of his name, including the Italian and Flemish versions, Orlando di Lasso and Rolande de Lattre. He probably began as a choirboy in his birthplace, Mons. Melodramatically, he was kidnapped on account of his beautiful voice and spirited off to Italy, where he soon entered the service of Ferdinand Gonzaga, and travelled widely, visiting Palermo, Naples and Milan. At twenty one he became choirmaster at St. John Lateran in Rome, but held the post only two years, returning to the Low Countries. After periods of travel in northern Europe, he was employed by the Duke of Bavaria in 1556, and remained attached to the Bavarian court for the rest of his life, though he was a frequent honoured guest in many capitals of Europe.

An extremely prolific composer, with well over one thousand two hundred works to his credit (including five hundred motets), Lassus displays an extraordinary mastery of all forms and styles of vocal music current in his day. It is hard to believe, for example, that the extrovert and ribald madrigal, *Matona mia cara*, the delicate French love song, *Mon coeur se recommande à vous*, and the highly chromatic and etherial *Prophetiae sibyllarum*, each a masterpiece in its own genre, all stem from the same pen. *Alma Redemptoris* was a favoured text of Lassus and was set four times, the other versions being two for six voices and one for eight. The present setting first appeared in 1597, and was published as no. 241 of the complete works, *Magnum opus musicum*, 1604 (transcribed from copy in British Library). As with many pieces by Lassus, it does not reveal the simplicity and melodiousness which is characteristic of a Palestrina (cf. the setting in volume 1 of this series), but yields much of its austere, haunting and complex beauty when it has been heard several times. Undeniably, the work is uneven, though with many fine moments, and it seems to have a personal application which may never yield its secrets. Set in a mixed style, the motet is filled with movement, and all five parts are usually fully employed, with the principal exception one passage, "virgo prius", where the texture is suitably lightened by the use of the top three voices only. There is a very notable piece of madrigalian word-painting where the mainly triadic invocation "succure" is followed by a literal fall on "cadenti" as each part loses its balance after a quaver rest, and trips down from a quaver, the mishap being emphasised by an A minor chord (bar 15). In other respects, the intentions of the piece are not always easy to fathom, and the constantly recurring ornamental cadences are a little puzzling. Modulation is also frequent and rather restless, though the mode and key are mainly Mixolydian and A major.

The biography of the greatest 16th century Italian composer, Giovanni Pierluigi da Palestrina (c.1525-94) is fortunately very well documented. His was also one of the few lives of musicians thought appropriate for an opera, since it is rich and varied, contains many setbacks, and includes two marriages, for one of which he renounced his priestly vows. Palestrina spent most of his musical life in Rome, and held several important positions: as chapel master of the Julian choir, then of St. John Lateran and Santa Maria Maggiore, though a plan to make him chapel master of the Pontifical Choir under Sixtus V proved abortive. His range of publications is formidable, including ninety four masses, about four hundred motets, twelve lamentations and no fewer than thirty settings of the Magnificat. Even more amazing is the high standard that prevails throughout his works, though he nods occasionally, as in some of his masses. Five-part motets are especially popular with Palestrina, since he provided at least one hundred and seventy four.

Though Palestrina rarely resorts to dramatic or madrigalian devices in his sacred music, the *Canite tuba* is a welcome exception (part one of the tenth motet in *Motettorum . . . liber secundus*, Venice, 1572, copy in the Liceo Musicale, Bologna). It begins with a fanfare for three voices to be answered by a fanfare for four, followed by all voices for the homophonic statement that the Lord is at hand ("quia prope est"). The exclamation, "ecce venit", is made in extended notes with a quickened tempo and melisma for "salvandum". The crooked being made straight ("erunt prava") is repeated antiphonally, each time the crookedness being shown by syncopation, and the straightness by coincidence with the tactus, while the rough places being made smooth ("et aspera") is given a haunting downward progression of six-three chords. Then comes the high-lying invocation "veni Domine", which is worked through and developed in varying combinations of voices. Finally, there is a climactic peal of alleluias, sustaining the excitement of the motet to the very end. The second part of this double motet is *Rorate Coeli,* published separately by Chester.

The next composer, Robert Ramsey, is both the latest and the least known of those in this volume. Not even his birth and death dates have been discovered, though recent guesses hazard a lifespan of c.1590-c.1644. All that is known with certainty is that after seven years of study he took his Mus. B. at Cambridge in 1616; that he was organist of Trinity College, Cambridge, 1628-44; and master of the children there, 1637-44. His extant music, which is entirely vocal and mainly sacred, comprises services, anthems, motets, a few madrigals, canons, songs, and *In guiltie night,* a dialogue between Saul and the Witch of Endor. Much of Ramsey's sacred music, including *O sapientia* (thought to date between 1620 and 1630), is housed among the Peterhouse manuscripts in the University of Cambridge Library (two sets of part-books). The motet is fairly traditional in form, even in its handling of the Dorian mode, and is obviously intended to be *a capella.* It seems to reflect continental influence from about the last two decades of the 16th century, notably from the Roman and Venetian Schools, possibly with a touch of Handl. These influences are apparent in the handling of homophony and the mixed style, and in the antiphonal deployment of forces. The only hint of the early 17th century style of sacred music lies in the melodic use of the minor sixth both rising and falling (e.g., Bass, bars 2 - 3 and Cantus, bars 39 - 40) and diminished intervals (e.g., a diminished fourth, Quintus, bar 37). Among the most successful features of the motet is the convincing recreation of mood and the smooth movement from section to section.

One of the many remarkable things about William Byrd (1543-1623), the first composer in the Christmas section, is the freedom with which he was permitted not only to write but to publish so much Latin church music of the Roman Rite, and in fact he obtained a monopoly of music printing. That he was given so much latitude is a strong indication of how highly he was esteemed by the Queen, who although a great patroness of the arts, nevertheless gave ready assent to ever-mounting anti-Catholic legislation. He was even for a time organist of the Chapel Royal, holding the initial appointment jointly with his teacher and close friend, Thomas Tallis. Neither does Byrd seem to have surrendered his Catholicism, for he was frequently cited as a recusant, and he gave liberally of his friendship and aid to missionary priests. including Robert Southwell and Henry Garnet. His closeness to the spirituality of the Roman liturgy is reflected throughout his Latin music, motets and masses alike, though he was also a pioneer in the shaping of the tradition of Anglican Church music. Coupled with Byrd's copiousness and musical integrity is his great sense of variety and imagination, for he repeats himself remarkably infrequently and can respond to virtually any liturgical text.

Byrd's *Beata viscera,* is the eleventh motet in his *Gradualia,* Book I (transcribed from the copy of the second edition in the British Library), being one of six five-part settings for the feast of the Nativity of Our Lady. The text is also the seventh responsory for the office of Christmas, hence its inclusion here. A remarkably gentle and beautiful motet, somewhat in the Roman style of polyphony, its melodic lines are delicately pointed and dovetail perfectly before coming gently to rest on "Filium". As frequently happens in Byrd, the final alleluia is completely separate, though it perfectly matches the mood of the main section in its expression of quiet joy. The mode is transposed Hypoaeolian, but frequently moves into the related key of D major.

Francesco Corteccia (1504-71) is the earliest composer in this collection. He was born in Arezzo, and became first organist at the church of San Lorenzo in Florence. Then he held the prestigious appointment of maestro di cappella to Duke Cosimo, the great patron of the arts, for whom he composed special wedding music. Among his varied other compositions, many of which have not survived, are three books of madrigals and musical intermezzi to stage plays.

His sacred music includes a set of responsories and lessons (1570) and *Canticorum liber primus*, published posthumously in Venice in 1571, from which the present work, *Surge illuminare Jerusalem*, the first part of a double motet, is taken (copy in Augsberg Staatsbibliothek). Corteccia resembles Palestrina in his simple beauty of melody and the smoothness and ease of both his fugal and mixed styles of writing. Indeed, Palestrina's eight-part setting (1575), though more spacious and on a much larger scale, seems to derive some of the melodic concepts from it. Corteccia relies little on adornment: melismas are rare and word-painting is confined to very brief touches, as in the opening leap of a fifth in all parts for "Surge". He does, however, make much use of text repetition, with a layering effect achieved by accumulative entries for each voice, especially appropriate in the final section beginning "et gloria Domuni".

The Spanish composer, Juan Esquivel, flourished at the beginning of the 17th century. He was a pupil of Juan Navarro, and succeeded him as chapel master at Ciudad Rodrigo. He was patronised by the bishop of the diocese, Pedro de Leon, who subsidised his publications, which included a volume of masses (1608), motets for four, five, six and eight voices (1608), and a lost volume of psalms, hymns, antiphons and masses (1613). Works also survive in manuscript.

His *Tria sunt munera* was first published in *Motecta festorum et dominicarum*, 1608 (copy in the library of the Hispanic Society of America). It bears out the commonly held notion that Esquivel is a conservative composer, even to the point of consistent and orthodox use of a plainsong *cantus firmus*, sung here by the Superius 2. The use of mode is also quite cautious until near the end, and it seems likely that Esquivel even preferred the rules of *musica ficta* to be applied very sparingly, to judge from the way accidentals are supplied in the printed text (cf. Superius I, bar 5). For all its conservatism, the motet is effective, pleasant and unobvious, and has an interesting and continuous movement.

Peter Philips (1561-1628) is still a comparatively neglected composer, though he made a significant impact in many areas of music, including motets (one volume for five voices and one for eight), sacred songs with accompaniment, hymns, madrigals, and instrumental music. A big obstacle in editing his music is that in some cases part books are missing: in one instance, a whole book of masses has been lost. Philips began as a choirboy at St. Paul's, then fled to the continent as a Catholic exile in 1582. He spent the rest of his life abroad, where he served as a musician at the English College, Rome, under Felice Anerio for three years (1582-5), and then he was chief musician to Lord Thomas Paget, one of the most prominent and influential of the English Catholic exiles, travelling with him widely, especially in Italy, France, Spain and the Low Countries. When Paget died in 1590, Philips earned his living by teaching the keyboard in Antwerp. In 1597 he became organist to the Archduke Albert at the Royal Chapel in Brussels, and stayed in that post until his death in 1628. The Royal Chapel was one of the most impressive centres for music at the time, and almost had a monopoly of the finest organists in Europe. Philips was an active member of a cultural circle of English exiles. He even followed the current religious polemics avidly — understandably, because he took holy orders in 1610 and became a canon. He also kept in contact with many leading composers, including Sweelinck, whom he visited.

Philips's *O beatum et sacrosanctum diem* (probably the only known Renaissance setting of this text) is a sparkling Christmas piece with a wide range of moods and effects, and deserves to become as secure a favourite in the Christmas repertoire as the Sweelinck, which bears some affinity to it, especially in the final section. It was published in *Cantiones sacrae quinis vocibus*, Antwerp, Pierre Phalèse, 1612 (transcribed from the British Library copy). In general style it is, like the other motets in the collection, somewhat transitional between Roman polyphony of the late 16th century and Early Baroque of the Venetian School, with a few parallel features of contemporary German and Slovene polyphony. As if recognizing the transition himself, Philips added a *basso continuo* in his second edition of the *Cantiones*, 1617 (published here from the British Library copy) though it is mainly a simple *basso seguente*.

Set in the bright Ionian mode (virtually C major, transposed here to B♭ major) it moves briskly and brightly in homophonic and antiphonal style throughout, with each section clearly separated. The opening, however, is gently devotional to express the wonderment of the moment, beginning with three voices, with the alto added halfway through the statement (cf. Philip's *Tibi Laus*, volume 9). The bass is reserved for the full-voice ensemble in triple time in the rejoicing of Gaudeat". The speed then doubles with a profusion of quavers and leads into a silvery fanfare of trumpets, as the three top parts move down the triad in *stretto* canon, the tenor matching the rhythm on mainly the tonic and dominant, while the bass has a form of anchoring pedal point. Word-painting is continued for the quick plucking semiquavers of "cithara", with a few suggestive touches also for "psalterio et organo". The bass then leads into the new section of rejoicing, which begins with a quick pattern for "multitudine angelorum" followed by two slower sections (in the style of Viadana) as if the brakes have to be applied for a breathing space before the finale (cf. *Tibi Laus*, bars 60-2). The conclusion, a flurry of "noës" or "alleluias" (the alternative provided in the original), is an exciting variation on the "in sono tubae", but with even the bass springing into life in the breathlessly exciting paean of joy.

In addition to its intrinsic value, *O beatum* is of considerable musicological interest, in that it contains many of the characteristic traits of Philips (cf. especially *Tibi Laus*, already cited, and *Ascendit Deus*, which has a similar section for "in sono tubae"), but it also seems part of a chain of influences. For example, as Kenneth Long has noted (*Music of the English Church*, 1972, p. 191), the "in sono tubae" section seems to derive from Jacob Handl's *Ascendit Deus*, while Sweelinck's *Hodie Christus natus est* owes some inspiration to the "noë" section.

Jan Pieterzoon Sweelinck (1562-1621) ends this collection with a suitable flourish. He seems to have spent most of his life in Amsterdam where his reputation as an organist was as great as for his compositions. He was however alive to the different developments in vocal music in other centres of Europe, not only by studying them in available printed texts, but by discussions and exchanges such as the one that took place between him and his friend Peter Philips in 1593. Sweelinck's publications in secular and sacred music are copious and contributed to the development of new vocal melody and rhythm, while his organ compositions greatly advanced the keyboard fugue, especially in converting the pedal into an intrinsic part of the fugal structure.

Sweelinck's *Hodie Christus natus est* is no. 13 of *Cantiones sacrae cum basso continuo ad organum* which was printed by Philips's publisher Pierre Phalèse (possibly with Philips's help) in Antwerp in 1619 (copy in the Bibliothèque Nationale, Paris). It is an excitingly dramatic piece, but, although not a particularly long work, is also one of the most tiring and difficult to sing well, being especially taxing in *tessitura* for all parts. Lowering the high *chiavette* by one tone seems to be most satisfactory means of accommodating all the parts, though reinforcing the altos with tenors or counter-tenors may then be necessary.

The piece is too famous to require much in the way of stylistic description. Like the Philips motet, it combines traditional and new features in a very convincing synthesis, uses a wide range of note values and tempi, and also includes a *basso continuo*. Sweelinck is especially adept in unifying the work through the recurrent use of theme and its inversion as has been noted by Gustave Reese (*Music in the Renaissance,* 1959, p. 518), and skilfully portrays the text through imaginative word-painting, notably in "in terra canunt angeli", where the angels fly down and indulge in ornamented singing matches, while the archangels rejoice in triple time. Most impressive of all is the final section, where, as in Dering's *Quem vidistis* (published separately by Chester) the earth and sky are gradually filled with sounds of exultation. It has been stated above that Sweelinck seems to imitate the Philips *O beatum* in its final climax of "noe, alleluia". But it is also important to note that Sweelinck imitates as any good Renaissance artist: he borrows out of deference, and then creates a new whole undeniably his own.

Table of use according to the Tridentine rite

Motet	liturgical source	seasonal or festal use
Orietur stella	2nd responsory, Wednesday, 3rd week of Advent	Advent
Alma Redemptoris	antiphon, Blessed Virgin, Advent to Purification	Advent to Purification
Canite tuba	antiphon 1 & 3, Vespers, 4th Sunday of Advent	Advent
O sapientia	great antiphon, 17th December	Advent, Pentecost
Beata viscera	7th responsory, Matins of Christmas	Christmas, Blessed Virgin
Surge illuminare Jerusalem	2nd lesson, Matins of Epiphany	Epiphany, Christmas
Tria sunt munera	antiphon, Benedictus, Tuesday of Epiphany week	Epiphany, Christmas
O beatum et sacrosanctum diem	antiphon, Christmas, Old Office	Christmas
Hodie Christus natus est	antiphon, Magnificat, Christmas	Christmas